SOUTHERN IS...

BY MARY NORTON KRATT

ILLUSTRATED BY BILL DRATH

Peachtree Publishers, Ltd.

Published by
PEACHTREE PUBLISHERS, LTD.
494 Armour Circle, N.E.
Atlanta, Georgia 30324

20 19 18 17 16 15 14 13 12 11

Library of Congress Catalog Number 85-60340

ISBN: 0-931948-68-1

To
Edna Faye, Mary Ruth,
Tammy Sue, Lucy Margaret, Mary Caroline,
and all Southern women
who have always worn double names.

SOUTHERN IS---

THERE'S NOTHING VERY DIFFERENT ABOUT SOUTHERNERS—
EXCEPT FOR THE WAY THEY THINK AND FEEL AND ACT.

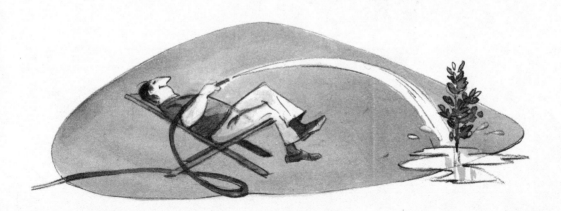

SOUTHERN IS KNOWING WHERE YOUR PEOPLE CAME FROM,

HOW THEY GOT THERE, WHERE THEY'RE BURIED,
AND WHO MARRIED WHO —
OR SHOULD'VE AND DIDN'T.

SOUTHERN IS CALLING HER MISS OLIVIA
BECAUSE EVERYBODY ELSE DOES,

OR COLONEL BECAUSE HE'S SAID TO HAVE SERVED,

OR JUDGE BECAUSE HE ACTS LIKE ONE.

SOUTHERN IS PATIENCE—

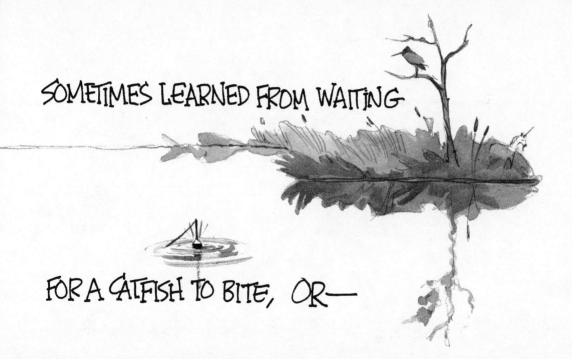

SOMETIMES LEARNED FROM WAITING

FOR A CATFISH TO BITE, OR—

FOR YOUR BROTHER TO PASS THE FRIED CHICKEN, OR—

FROM LISTENING TO UNCLE WILL SAY A TEN-MINUTE BLESSING.

SOUTHERN IS KNOWING THAT A TICKING,

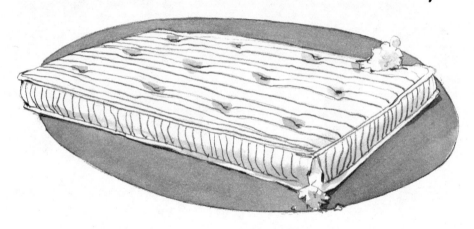

A TICK,

ARE ALTOGETHER THREE ENTIRELY DIFFERENT THINGS.

SOUTHERN IS HAVING THREE THOROUGHLY
ECCENTRIC COUSINS—

LIKE MAUDE, WHO ALL HER LIFE
WORE BLACK STOCKINGS
AND A PLAIT DOWN HER BACK
AND WALKED FOR THE MAIL

DOWN THE YELLOW LINE ON THE HIGHWAY;

OR LIKE COUSIN SEBRON, WHO WAS ALWAYS
BURYING HIS MONEY UNDER ONE
SWEET GUM TREE OR ANOTHER ;

OR—
LIKE OLD MIZ GUTHRIE, WHOSE HOUSE SMELLED SWEET
AND WET LIKE MILDEWED VANILLA AND WHO NEVER
THREW ANYTHING AWAY.

SOUTHERN IS KNOWING WHAT THEY'RE TALKING ABOUT

WHEN A MENU OFFERS

HOMINY GRITS,
LIVERMUSH,
POKE SALLAT,
CREASYS,
COLLARDS

AND CRACKLIN' CORN BREAD.

IT'S ALSO MEANING IT
SOMETIMES
AND SERVING THE
BEST LIQUOR
AND SAYING
"DON'T GO"—MEANING
ANOTHER HOUR'D BE OK
IF YOU CAN TELL A
FEW MORE GOOD STORIES.

SOUTHERN IS CONSTANTLY DROPPIN' YOUR Gs

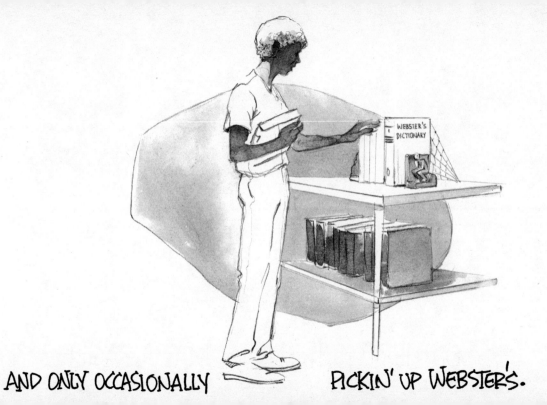

AND ONLY OCCASIONALLY PICKIN' UP WEBSTER'S.

SOUTHERN IS THINKING THAT A BAGEL—

IS A HUNTING DOG.

SOUTHERN IS REMEMBERING KINDNESSES
AND NURTURING HATREDS —

OR TRANSCENDING HATREDS AND TRYING OUT KINDNESSES,
EVEN WHEN IT'S AWFUL UNCOMFORTABLE.

SOUTHERN IS LIKING SMALL WOMEN
WITH SOFT VOICES

AND IRON INSIDE—

AND ADMIRING MEN WHO
OPEN DOORS FOR YOU

AND GRASP YOUR ELBOW
WHEN YOU COME TO A CURB.

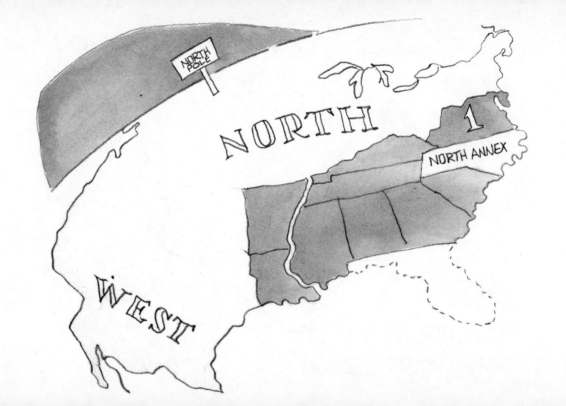

SOUTHERN IS THINKING CAROLINA IS NORTH,
VIRGINIA IS FIRST,
FLORIDA IS NOT,
TEXAS IS WEST,
AND THE NINETEENTH CENTURY IS NEW.

SOUTHERN IS KNOWING A WOMAN
WHO HAS MADE
A CAREER

OUT OF BEING
A LADY.

SOUTHERN IS MAKING BUTTERMILK BISCUITS FOR BREAKFAST

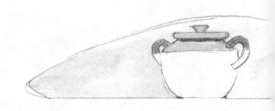

BEFORE YOU'RE HALF AWAKE;

BELIEVING GOOD BARBECUE

IS HIGH CULINARY ART;

AND TAKING FOOD
TO A HOME WHERE THERE'S BEEN A DEATH,

EVEN IF NOBODY'S HUNGRY OR GONNA BE.

BEING SOUTHERN IS THINKING OF CHURCH AS A HABIT,
LIKE PUTTING ON SHOES OR SETTING YOUR CLOCK;

SOUTHERN IS GROWING UP WITH BLACK DIRT OR
RED CLAY UNDERFOOT AND KNOWING FOR CERTAIN
THAT THOSE WERE THE ONLY COLORS
THE EARTH COULD BE.

SOUTHERN IS SEEING OLD PLANTATION HOUSES
AT THE END OF LONG, TREE-LINED LANES

AND KNOWING THAT NOBODY IN YOUR FAMILY
EVER LIVED LIKE THAT—

BUT SECRETLY WISHING.

SOUTHERN IS KNOWING FOR CERTAIN THAT
YOU'RE SPECIAL —
AND NOT REALLY EVER BEIN' SURE WHY.

MARY NORTON KRATT was born in West Virginia but has spent most of her life in the lowlands of North Carolina. A graduate of Agnes Scott College, Ms. Kratt has been published in numerous newspapers, magazines and literary journals, including *Southern Review*, *Southern Poetry Review*, *South Carolina Review* and the *International Poetry Review*. Her first collection of poems, *Spirit Going Barefoot*, was published in 1982. She lives with her family in Charlotte, North Carolina.

Although illustrator BILL DRATH grew up in Wisconsin, he had the good sense to marry a Southerner and consequently has spent many years south of the Mason-Dixon line. His drawings have been highly acclaimed, and his watercolors in *If I Found A Wistful Unicorn* have helped to make that book an enduring best seller. Drath, a retired lieutenant colonel from the U.S. Army, now is a free-lance illustrator and lives with his wife Sara in Atlanta, Georgia.